BLACK BEARS

by Tammy Gagne

AMICUS HIGH INTEREST AMICUS INK

Amicus High Interest and Amicus Ink
are imprints of Amicus
P.O. Box 1329, Mankato, MN 56002
www.amicuspublishing.us

Library of Congress Cataloging-in-Publication Data

Gagne, Tammy, author.
 Black bears / by Tammy Gagne.
     pages cm. -- (Wild bears)
 "Amicus High Interest is published by Amicus."
 Summary: "Presents information about black bears living in North
America, their habitats, and their sharp senses."-- Provided by publisher.
 Includes bibliographical references and index.
 ISBN 978-1-60753-773-1 (library binding)
 ISBN 978-1-60753-872-1 (ebook)
 ISBN 978-1-68152-024-7 (paperback)
 1. Black bear--Juvenile literature. [1. Bears.] I. Title.
 QL737.C27G32 2014
 599.78'5--dc23
                          2014043592

Photo Credits: Ken Hoehn/iStock/Thinkstock, cover; Debbie Steinhausser/
Shutterstock Images, 2, 4–5, 19, 23; iStockphoto/Thinkstock, 6–7; Gerald
Marella/Shutterstock Images, 8–9; Jason Crader/iStock/Thinkstock, 10;
Wild Art/Shutterstock Images, 12–13; RONSAN4D/iStock/Thinkstock,
14–15, 22; Peter Bisset/Stock Connection/Glow Images, 16–17; Menno
Schaefer/Shutterstock Images, 20–21

Produced for Amicus by The Peterson Publishing Company
and Red Line Editorial.

Designer Becky Daum
Printed in Malaysia

HC 10 9 8 7 6 5 4 3 2 1
PB 10 9 8 7 6 5 4 3 2 1

TABLE OF CONTENTS

BLACK BEAR HABITATS

Black bears are common in
North America. They live in
many different **habitats**. Some
roam in forests. Others live on
mountains.

COLOR AND SIZE

Most black bears have black fur. But some are brown or blonde. Their size varies. Bears in the north are larger. They weigh up to 900 pounds (409 kg).

Fun Fact
A few black bears have white fur. They are known as spirit bears.

CLIMBING AND SWIMMING

Black bears are big. But they are not slow. Black bears are fast. They can climb trees. They are good swimmers too.

Fun Fact
A black bear can outrun the fastest person.

AVOIDING DANGER

Black bears escape danger quickly.

They run away if they are surprised.

They climb up a tree. Some even

run away from butterflies.

SHARP SENSES

Black bears have great eyes and noses. This helps them find food. They also have good memories. They remember where food is.

BLACK BEAR FOOD

Black bears eat fish. They also eat plants. The bears find berries and nuts. Some even eat insects. They eat ants and termites.

WINTER

Food is hard to find in the cold.
Black bears **hibernate** in winter.
The bears climb into a **den**. They
stay still for months. Their hearts
beat slower. This lets them live
without eating.

RAISING CUBS

Black bear babies are called cubs. Cubs stay with their mothers for up to two years. Fathers do not help raise cubs. Adults spend most of their lives alone.

Fun Fact

Cubs are born blind. Their eyes are closed. They open their eyes after one month.

GROWING IN NUMBERS

Black bears live in large territories. About 600,000 of them live in the wild. Other bears have become rare. But black bear numbers are growing.

Fun Fact
People are the only predators black bears have.

BLACK BEAR FACTS

Size: 86–901 pounds (39–409 kg), 47–79 inches (120–200 cm)

Range: North America

Habitat: forests, mountains, swamps

Number of babies: 2

Food: fish, berries, nuts, insects

WORDS TO KNOW

den – a hole or cave where an animal lives

habitats – places where plants or animals naturally live

hibernate – to pass the winter in a resting state

predators – things that hunt or eat other animals

LEARN MORE

Books

Daly, Timothy M. *Black Bears*. New York: Scholastic, 2012.

Kolpin, Molly. *American Black Bears*. Mankato, Minn.: First Facts, 2011.

Swinburne, Stephen R. *Black Bear: North America's Bear*. Honesdale, Penn.: Boyds Mill Press, 2009.

Websites

Defenders of Wildlife—Black Bears Fact Sheet
http://www.defenders.org/black-bear/basic-facts
Learn more about what black bears eat and how they behave.

National Geographic—Black Bears
http://animals.nationalgeographic.com/animals/mammals/black-bear
See many photos of black bears in the wild.

INDEX